No Rhyme No Reason

Searching for Equanimity

Bala Mudaly

An Anthology of Poems

No Rhyme, No Reason
© Bala Mudaly 2025

ISBN: 978-1-7638368-3-9

Tale

Cover design by Robert New

Names, characters and events are the products of the author's imagination. Any resemblance to actual persons, living or dead, or actual events is purely coincidental.

Tale Publishing Melbourne, Australia

Truth is elusive, concealed between myth and reality

Dedication

To the enduring courage and sacrifice of poets, writers, journalists and advocates of free speech in a world fraught with human right abuses and democracy in seeming retreat.

Introduction

'A poem should not *mean* but simply *be*.'
Archibald MacLeish

Does poetry matter? It matters to me as a concise way to express/explore my largely fleeting thoughts and feelings about events in my life, in my unfolding world.

On reflection, it seems early memories are more readily accessible to me in old age than very recent ones. It's as if my past is etched in stone while my present drifts away on water, the memories of these days evaporating in the sun.

Stray lines of poetry, lines learnt *by heart* in my school years some eighty years ago, often pop up into my consciousness, intrusive as ghosts that haunt people's dreams.

- *I wandered lonely as a cloud...*
- *Under a spreading chestnut tree, the village smithy stands...*

- *I must down to the sea again, to the lonely sea and sky...*

- *Is there anybody there? Said the traveller, knocking on the moonlit door...*

In recent years, I've tried my hand at writing poetry but have kept them largely private. This is because I'm somewhat daunted by poetry. I wish someone would explain what makes poetry, *poetry*. In fact, I view published poems with respectful awe, especially where their intended meaning and purpose seem intentionally elusive. Much of contemporary poetry appears to be a radical departure from traditional, classical forms with which I grew up at school and university. Writing poetry as a personal pursuit is one thing, but to invite the public to read them is quite something else. It requires some measure of courage and confidence. While I may read and readily express an opinion on a book or short story, I hesitate to do so with poetry. It's just that I can't seem to tell what's acceptable and what's not, especially since free verse has become so popular.

Perhaps there's no such thing as *good or bad* poetry. It's all a matter of personal taste. Beauty, they say, is in the eye of the beholder. I have attended a few poetry slam sessions in Melbourne where budding poets take to the stage and recite their latest poems to a live audience, who then offer spontaneous feedback. Often, when the poet reads his creative attempt aloud, all his intended elements in verse (such as meaning, and rhythm) became clearer, thereby enabling the audience to enjoy and appreciate the poem that much more, both at an emotional and intellectual level.

Now, I've finally decided to produce a collection of my own poems, even though the collection will always remain a *work-in-progress*. The poems are presented in three clusters under the headings *Take Your Pick, This Passing Life,* and *It Is What It Is*. The clustering is somewhat arbitrary and may be ordered under other themes. In any case, I now submit the collection to you, the reader, to make of them whatever you will. No doubt some poems will resonate more with you relative to your own personal experience and your understanding of poetry as a literary form. Others in this collection may leave you puzzled, cold or critical. That much I expect.

Contents

Introduction

Take Your Pick — 1

- Hippopotami — 3
- Growing Old — 4
- Homecoming — 5
- Way Forward — 6
- Big Ben Tolls A Queen's Passing — 7
- Gotta-move-on — 8
- Trash and Treasure — 9
- Happiness & Joy — 10
- Happy Mindless Mind — 11
- A Kind of Blindness — 12
- Trumpet Man — 13
- Path of Return — 14

This Passing Life — 15

- No More Tomorrows — 17
- If I come again — 18
- Impermanence — 19
- Make the Moment Last — 20
- Journey's End — 21
- Emptiness of Suffering — 22
- The Human Condition — 24
- Coriander — 25

Dare	26
Birds in Flight	27
Heaven and Earth	28
Tell Me Why	29
It is what it is	31
Lust for Killing	33
Second Coming*	35
Averted Gaze	36
Oh Guernica	37
Witness The Scream	39
Flanders Field	40
Extinction	41
What a piece of work is man	42
Rivers of Babylon	43
It Is What It is	44
Grant Me	45
Appreciation	47
Author Profile	49

Take Your Pick

Hippopotami

'What's new your way?' asked the ancient man
Dark against the mid-day sun.
'Hippopotami,' I replied,
Pointing the way I'd come.
Hippopotami?
Incredulity creased his bearded face
As he passed me by
On his tall camel
Chewing and nodding,
Giving me the evil eye.
The lurid sun whirled and swirled.
What's this thing *hippopotami*?
My camel snorted,
Felling me off my high seat
Into the sea of shifting sand
And bolted in disgust.

Growing Old

I grow old, grow old
Shrink and buckle a little each day
Wear the bottoms of my pyjamas rolled*
Hey, I keep my socks on 24/7
Since no one feels the cold as much as me
When icy winds blow and blow.
But when the heater's going ballistic
Cooling down is easy,
I just kick off one sock.
Right foot or left
Seems not to matter much.
It works for me
Every time
TS Eliot

Homecoming

Our individual and collective glory
Sung
We lay down our arms
Recede into the mass of
Faceless braves
Comrades all!
Past days of anguished pain,
Relentless memories of exile
In foreign lands
Overlaid now
With new pain, new uncertainties.
Comrades all,
Exiles again in a strange land,
Our Motherland!
We present a brave face
Harmonising together a different song:
'Happy days are here again...'

(Tribute to returning ANC combatants.
Published in *Staffrider* V9, N4 1991)

Way Forward

Often times the way forward
For humankind
Is never the straight and narrow
Flight of a black bird
To a promised new El Dorado
Far from blight and scarcity,
And dreams scattered.
The way forward is the arc of return
To the beginning
And seeing it anew, *
With the eye of Odysseus.
**TS Eliot*

Big Ben Tolls A Queen's Passing

Autumnal pageantry like no other
Draws out solemn crowds,
Crown worshippers
Spilling and weaving along London streets
Moving like passionate ants with purpose.
End of an era they say
Mother of Great Britain,
Commonwealth and realms.
Muffled gongs wrench emotions
Reverberations in mind and soul,
The old order's turning over
Foreshadowing an uncertain winter
The gloom of a long fall
I toll for you and you and you.

Gotta-move-on

We do it all the time,
It's called letting go,
Turning a new page,
Starting afresh
Making a new beginning
Shedding an accumulation of
Possessions and aggravations.
Dumping them willy-nilly on the nature strip
As trash.
There's no time to grieve, no time for second thoughts
No, not even a last anguished glance
At mum's endeared piano, dad's fishing rods
Kids' books and toys, teddy bears and trampoline
Outgrown, relegated, forgotten, unwanted
Musty with memories of long-lost joy.
Go now, travelling light
Taking just yourself
Your bitterness and resentments
Masked in nonchalance.

Trash and Treasure

You may well ask what's the difference
When trash and treasure
Are sides of the same coin,
Encirclement of an idea no more,
A presupposition.
Contemplate, too,
The still point of this turning world*
When comings and goings matter not.
And trash and treasure are equally
compostable
In the fullness of time
Like the whole of life

*TS Eliot

Happiness & Joy

Happiness is a rare thing,
A passing shower
On a parched land.
Joy is the face of sorrow
Caught in a shaft of sunlight
From a dark-laden sky.

Happy Mindless Mind

The mind exists
Not here, not there, not anywhere
But centred somewhere in me
In the now.
So how would that feel for you?
No, I cannot guess that
Conclusively
Not like a rolling stone shorn of moss
Nor like a puff of white cloud
Pink-laced and proud
Billowing and blowing away
Ever so slowly,
Incrementally
Across an eternal eye
Vastly blue, empty, surreal
Going nowhere in any hurry.
Let's say then that the
Question still stands,
Mindlessly so.

A Kind of Blindness

You there,
See
This here burnt fractured land
Is *Country*
Ancient beyond time.
See how
Ghost gums stand darkly still
Against a star-sprinkled sky,
Ochre-red gorges
In deep, deep mourning.
Creeks and river-beds dry
Show scars of past deluge
Where burnished spinifex clumps
Keep watch
Over us Mob,
Invisible to you
At the waterhole.
You careless bushwalker
Stomping regardless
Turning every mulga tree
Into a lavatory
Seeing nothing
Knowing nothing.

Trumpet Man

You're too much with yourself,
Night and day
Dawn to dusk
Trumpeting your name,
Flooding the zone
With chaos and consternation.
Are you just a tweet
A new normal
Madness personified
Or method in madness?
Only time will tell.

Path of Return

A to B for sure
Is the way forward,
Straight as the crow flies
Headed forth with purpose and hope.
Land a-hoy!
The mariner on masthead high
Calls out to his wily
Captain on deck below.
I see flora, I see fauna,
I see *terra nullius*
Across waters vast.
 If only someone cautioned
The master of the fleet
To applaud not his arrival
In a far-flung foreign land,
But defer jubilation until
Safely back home on *terra firma*.

This Passing Life

Still and silent sea
In flux and flow
Forever.

No More Tomorrows

As light and warmth recede
Into the deepening shadows of dusk,
Joy gives way to regret,
Sadness
For pleasures and pain that's done.
Night beckons
With a resolute finger
Turning me in stillness,
In acceptance
In hope of finality
Not to rise again
No sun reborn
No morning dew
No existential woes.
Just this
Once rare and precious life.

If I come again

If I come again
Will you consider,
Will you promise
To plant acorns with me
On the way to London,
Sit under a tree and
Sing songs of praise
To lost worlds,
Fly to John O'Groats to see the
Sunset
And be back in Brighton
For dinner?
Whatever!
Should I come again
For God's sake
Let's do something
Profound and meaningful,
Like sitting in the mid-day sun
At Hyde Park
Celebrating our last hurrah!

Impermanence

Should I be fully present
When this body is turned into ash
And scattered to the wind,
Then will I have
Witnessed it all
At the heart of
Impermanence.

Make the Moment Last

We'll arrive there
Soon enough,
Young like you
Or old like me.
So why hurry,
Why rush?
Make the moment last. *
Slow down,
You're moving too fast
You got to make the morning last.

*Simon & Garfunkel

Journey's End

You go searching for the place to be
Between reality and hope,
Laughter and sorrow
Between the push and pull
Of gravity,
The still point
In a turning world. *
A distant horizon
Between sea and sky.
At journey's end
You return
Empty-handed
To where you began
And find
Equanimity.

***TS Eliot**

Emptiness of Suffering

(Reflections at a Buddhist Meditation Retreat)

Listen! What do you hear
In the stillness of the night?
I hear but the sound
Of silence and emptiness!
And what do you see?
Ah! The tall shadow of Sayadaw
Cast by candlelight.
I see darkly visible hulks
Of sitting Yogis,
And gliding ghost-like
Walking meditators
Shrouded in
Awesome stillness.
Yet listen again:
What is it you hear?
Ah! From the depth of silence
Come mutterings
Of many minds,

Beginners' minds,
Silently enduring pain,
Stepping out on the arduous path
To Mount Kailash,
Where frozen winds howl and mock
Three days no end,
Relentless
Night and day
Across a Tibetan plateau.
Searing
Through fissures in my mind
Assailing the senses
As I sit and walk, walk and sit,
Through weary hours from sunrise to dusk.
Will a peaceful mind ever arise!
Ah! The emptiness of suffering.

The Human Condition

Is it a case of not wanting what I want?
Night and day alone craving for
company,
Hating being crowded out
By clamouring voices calling
Come, come can't you see we are one,
In it together always.
But that's not it, not it at all. *
 To spin in solitude
In solitary motion
Into here and out there
Is the beginning and end of it all.
TS Eliot

Coriander

A sprig of coriander
Is all she had
To place gently beside him,
Her dear man for fifty long years
Now cold and darkly still.
Coriander rich and green
Wafting heady smells
Of earth and heaven.
Her pale hand brushing aside
A wisp of ivory hair from
Eyes welling with grief
For a passing as inevitable
As the setting sun
At day's end.

Dare

The day will come
sooner than later
When I'm called to rest.
Is it then time for me to dare,
 Dare to shut down my laptop
Close my eyes
And contemplate the Camino
My 80 odd years journey
Over highs and lows
Arduous and joyous
To this point of arrival?
Recall now faces and encounters
Along the long walk,
Savour once more and last
 Memories both precious and painful
Before they're lost in the
Wash of time.

Birds in Flight

Birds in flight
Leave no trace behind,
So why should I?

Heaven and Earth

Christ has arisen,
Rising into the firmament
Eternally blue,
Hallelujah!
The Buddha
Sits still grounded as a rock
And enlightened.
Heaven and Earth
Are but one.

Tell Me Why

Oh man, tell me why
Inspiring songs
Make me want to cry.
Tell me why
Fractured morning light
On dew
Tugs at my heart.
And what's in *dusk-light*
That conjures in me
A depth of sadness?
No more time to linger
No more time to turn and gaze
My last
On this rare thing called *life*
As the inevitable draws me
Into the vast unknown.

It is what it is

"I will write peace on your wings, and you will fly all over the world,"

Sadako: Hiroshima Peace Memorial Park

Lust for Killing

Hear me out when I speak,
Not half-heartedly
Not with a half-hearted ear.
What I communicate is
Subtle as frankincense,
A whiff of the unburied in morning light
On the field of Philippi. *
I proclaim *massacres* from recorded time
And time before then
When a falling star created DNA
In the image of man
With the gift to self-destruct.
Hidden in the shadow of fallen ramparts.
I witnessed then
Rome delivered fair passage
By Neptune across the seas
To crush the skulls of babes
And rip out the proud heart of Carthage.
Cries and wailing wafted by the wind
Down centuries,
Falling like acid rain

On *First Nation* people
On Troy and Hiroshima
On Srebrenica and Mullivaikkal
And ancient Armenia
On the killing fields of Cambodia
Boipatong and Wounded Knee,
And indeed, on Gaza.

***Shakespeare*

Second Coming*

The magi of old
Followed the bright morning star
To Bethlehem
Bringing gifts of
Gold, frankincense and myrrh; **
A ritual also honoured by
Santa Biden sprouting horns,
Slouching toward the Holy Land
Lugging gifts of turkey
Stuffed full of lethal intent,
Hundred pounders gifted
With compliments of the USA

**WB Yeats*
*** Bible*

Averted Gaze

Come see, that's Picasso's *Guernica*
And that's the *Scream* by Munch
Art imitating life.
Oh no, not so
It's life that mimics art.
Enough, enough,
My patience's quite spent
With such mindless
Ivory-tower quibble
When Gaza burns
And Darfur is ground into dust
By marauding beasts
With fire-spouting sticks.

Oh Guernica

Tell me it's not true
That Cain killed Abel*
Abetted by a vengeful God.
So unleashing upon the world
Brother-on-brother violence
An unending orgy of killing.
Oh Guernica
I was there on Golgotha strewn with skulls,
Faultline between Palestine and Israel
Spread-eagled and desiccated
On electrified wire;
Eyes tethered, pried wide chameleon-like.
Horror to the right, horror to the left
Averting not my gaze,
Compelled to witness inhumanity at its finest,
Savagery *par excellence*.

Oh Guernica

What is humankind
But a deprived beast that has fed on itself
Down the ages
Even before Nineveh
Was put to sword.

*Bible

Witness The Scream

Frozen in arctic ice,
Petrified on the rock-face of ancient
Carthage.
Terror-stifled and stillborn
An unreal world
Drenched in vengeance,
Depravity in all its glory
C*ivilization* so-called
Asserting itself.
As God's chosen people
Stride towards a higher purpose
Raining drones and bellicose bombs,
Indiscriminate unchallenged
With superior glee,
While the world looks on appalled
And applauding.

Flanders Field

See how the poppies bloom*
In Flanders field turned rich with
Blood of slaughtered armies.
See how Flanders flowers flourish
In gleeful abundance
In colours crimson,
Bright scarlet and burgundy red,
Flourish on composted corpses
Of young men long gone
Everyone.

**John McCrae*

Extinction

Humankind squats
At the edge of madness
Like a vulture at dawn,
Eyeing the unabated sport of
Mutual slaughter,
Gorging on bloodied flesh
Stewing in the midday sun,
Pecking at bones of offspring.
Mankind
Revelling in savagery,
Blind to annihilation
Hurtling its way.

What a piece of work is man

What a piece of work is man *
How noble, how like a God
How heavenly is his smile
That masks supreme bestiality
Written into his DNA.
**Shakespeare*

Rivers of Babylon

There by the rivers of Babylon
We sat down and wept
When we remembered Zion *
There now by the rivers of Jordan
We sit us down
And weep for Palestine.
Who now the victims,
Who now the pursued and persecuted,
The crushed souls,
Crushed and pulverised into
The very dust that's now Gaza?
In earth's infinite unfolding
Will there be other reckonings
To come
At other times?
Bible

It is what it is

It is what it is
Might is right, power prevails.
So says the soothsayer.
Military campaigns,
Conquest, rape and plunder
Common as carrion flies
Down the corridors of time;
A kind of brutal madness that
Cancels cultures, languages and peoples,
Advances empires
Energises *civilisations* so-called
Creates mass employment
Spawns new lethal inventions
Boosts ill-gotten wealth of nations
Enables a *chosen people*
To rewrite history in its image.
There's no rhyme nor reason
Why it is what it is,
It just is.

Grant Me

Grant me an ounce less despair
An ounce more joy
Fortitude to endure
And equanimity in old age.

Appreciation

The poems in this collection were written and accumulated over several years. A few have since been included in other publications of mine. In this incubation period, draft versions have been read and commented on by close friends and by members of writers' groups I've participated in. My sincere thanks for their invaluable feedback. Doug Wroe, Naleeza Ebrahim, Kieran Carroll and Robert New, however, deserve special mention for their unstinting editorial support. Sorry for leaning on you, guys. But then, what are loyal friends for!

Author Profile

Bala Mudaly, now in his late 80s, is retired and lives in Melbourne. Having endured fifty years of racial persecution in South Africa under apartheid, Bala and his wife immigrated to Australia in 1988. Reading, writing, gardening and walking the neighbourhood streets nurture and sustain him in his twilight years.

Other books by the author

www.ingramcontent.com/pod-product-compliance
Lightning Source LLC
Chambersburg PA
CBHW061731070526
44583CB00024B/3094